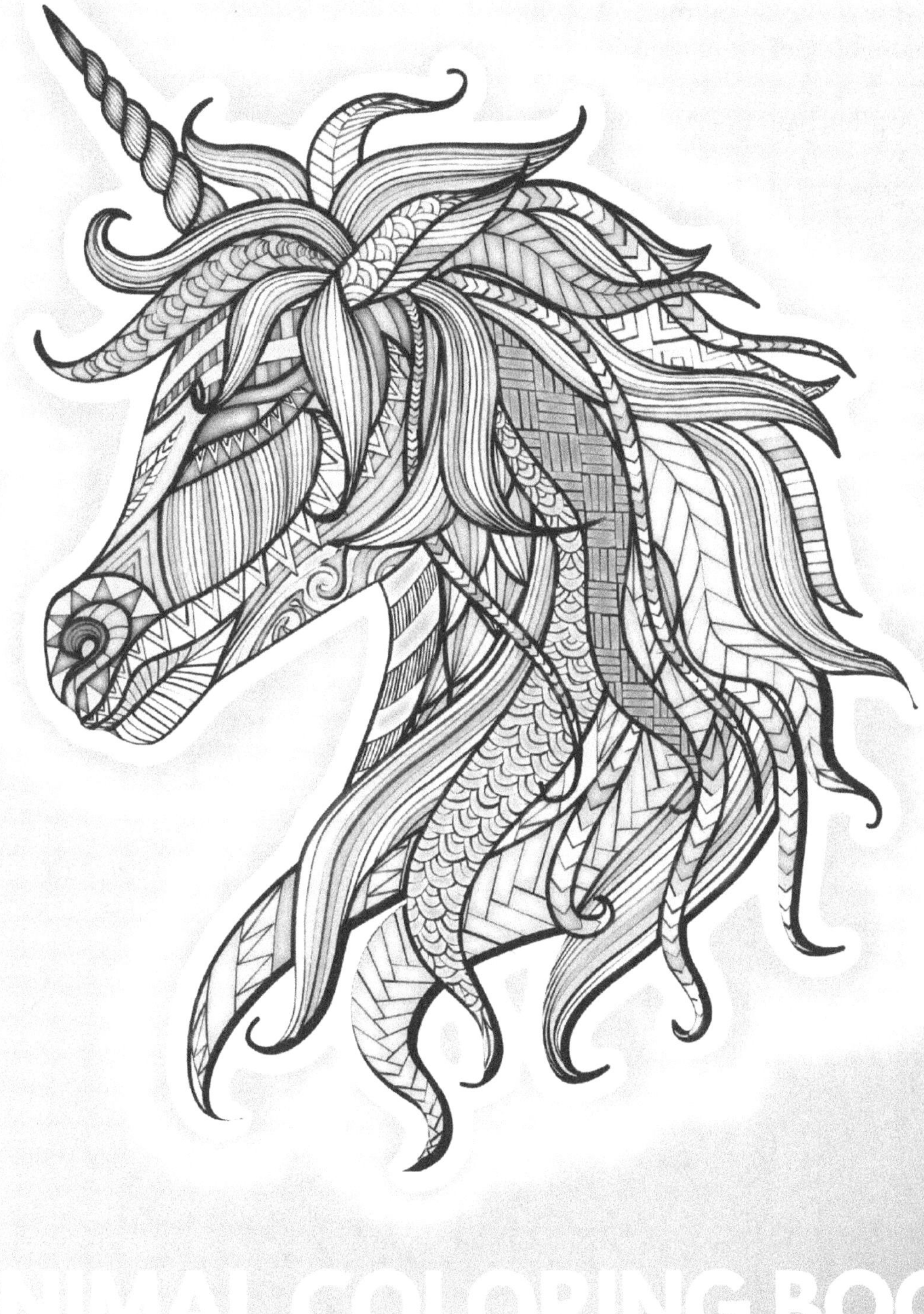

ANIMAL COLORING BOOK
FOR ADULTS

Printed in the United States of America

First Printing, 2019

ISBN 9781702342988

A Special Request

This book was made with care and lots of work. Just the fact that you chose to buy my book, out of all the other possible books you could have bought, means everything to me. If you got the time to review the book, on the platform where you bought it, that would be the greatest gift you could give me. Thank you!

Sincerely,

Autumn F.

-Tear out page-

Tear out this page and place underneath the page you are coloring if needed to avoid bleed-through.

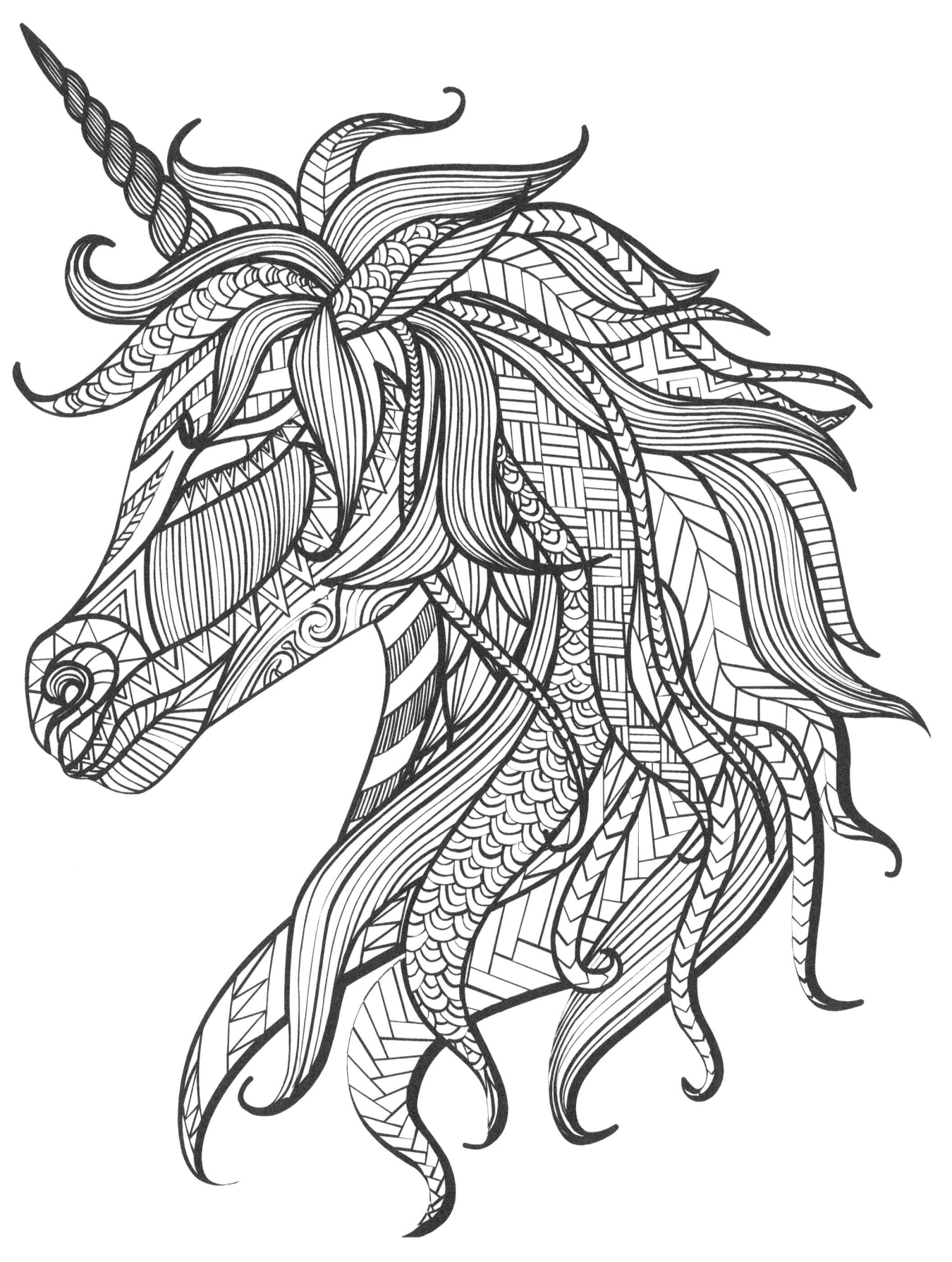

Intentionally blank

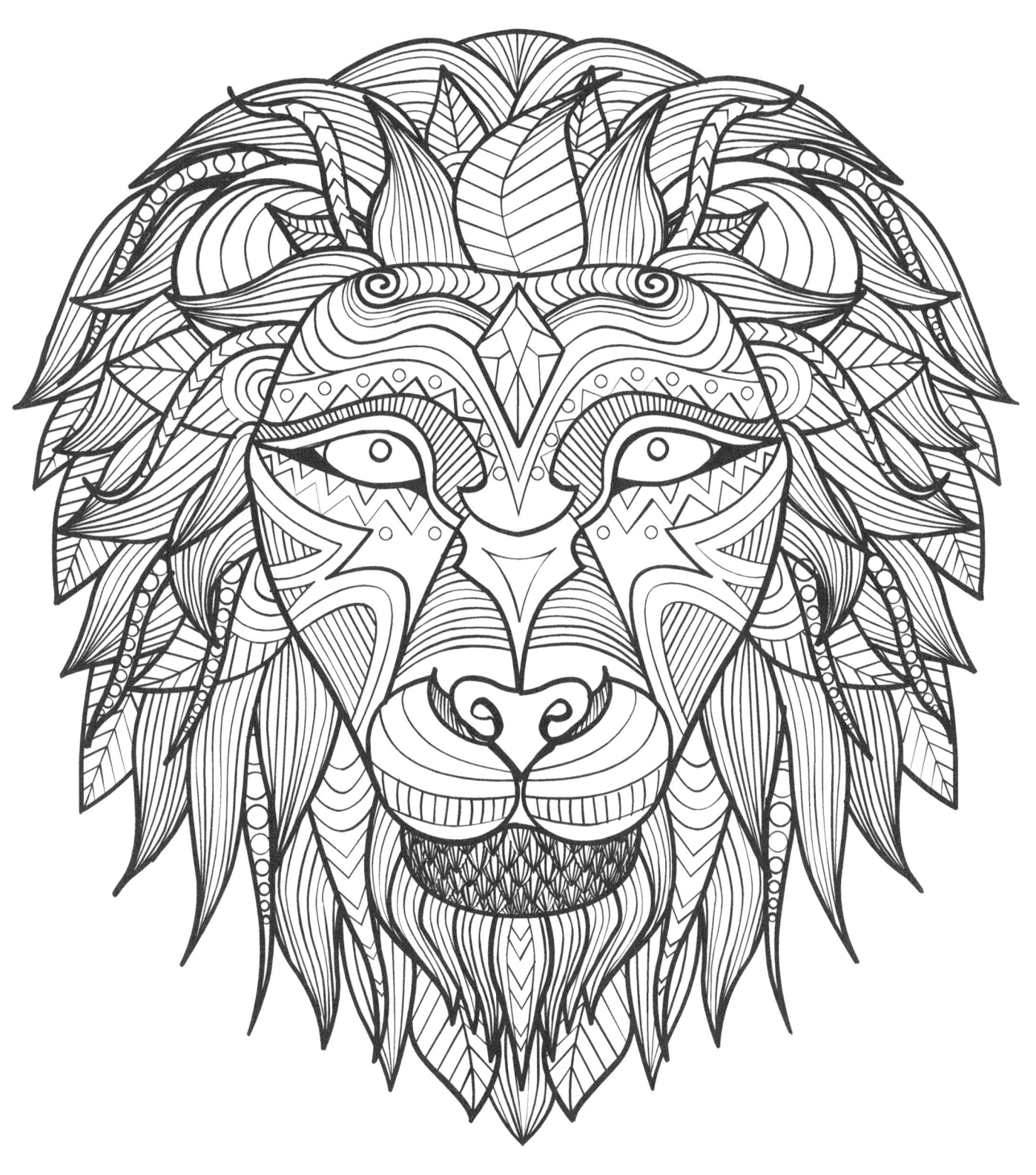

Intentionally blank

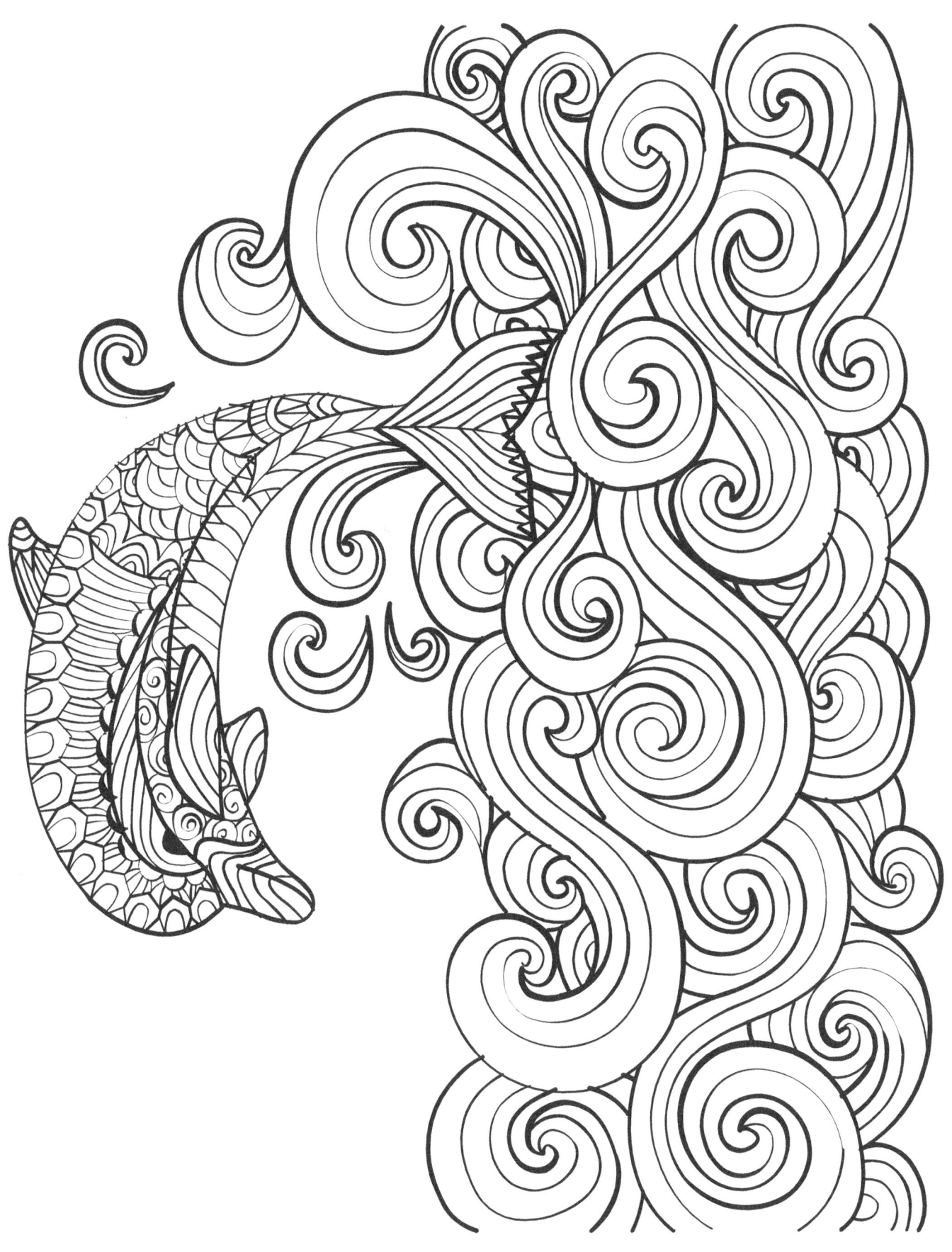

Intentionally blank

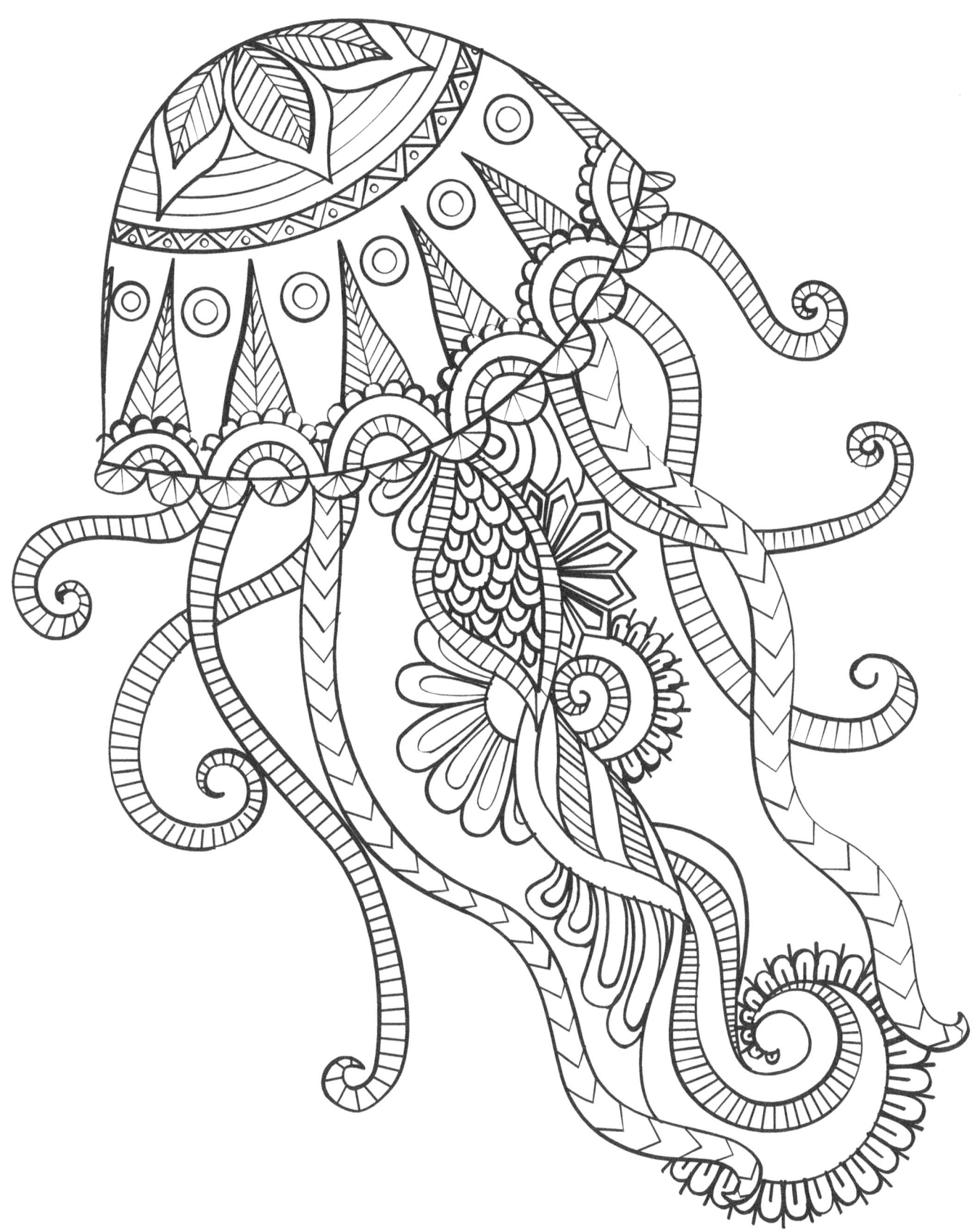

Intentionally blank

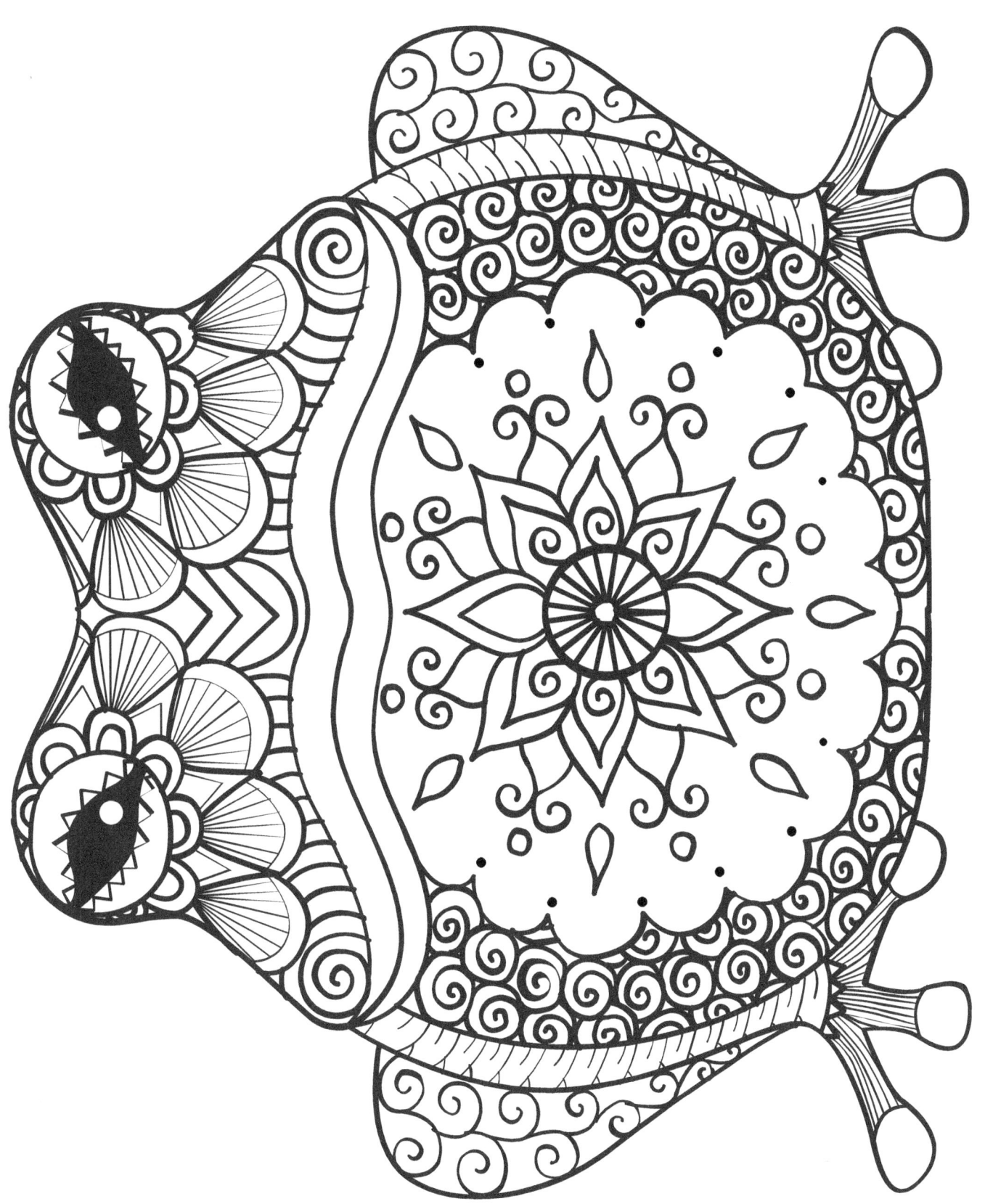

Intentionally blank

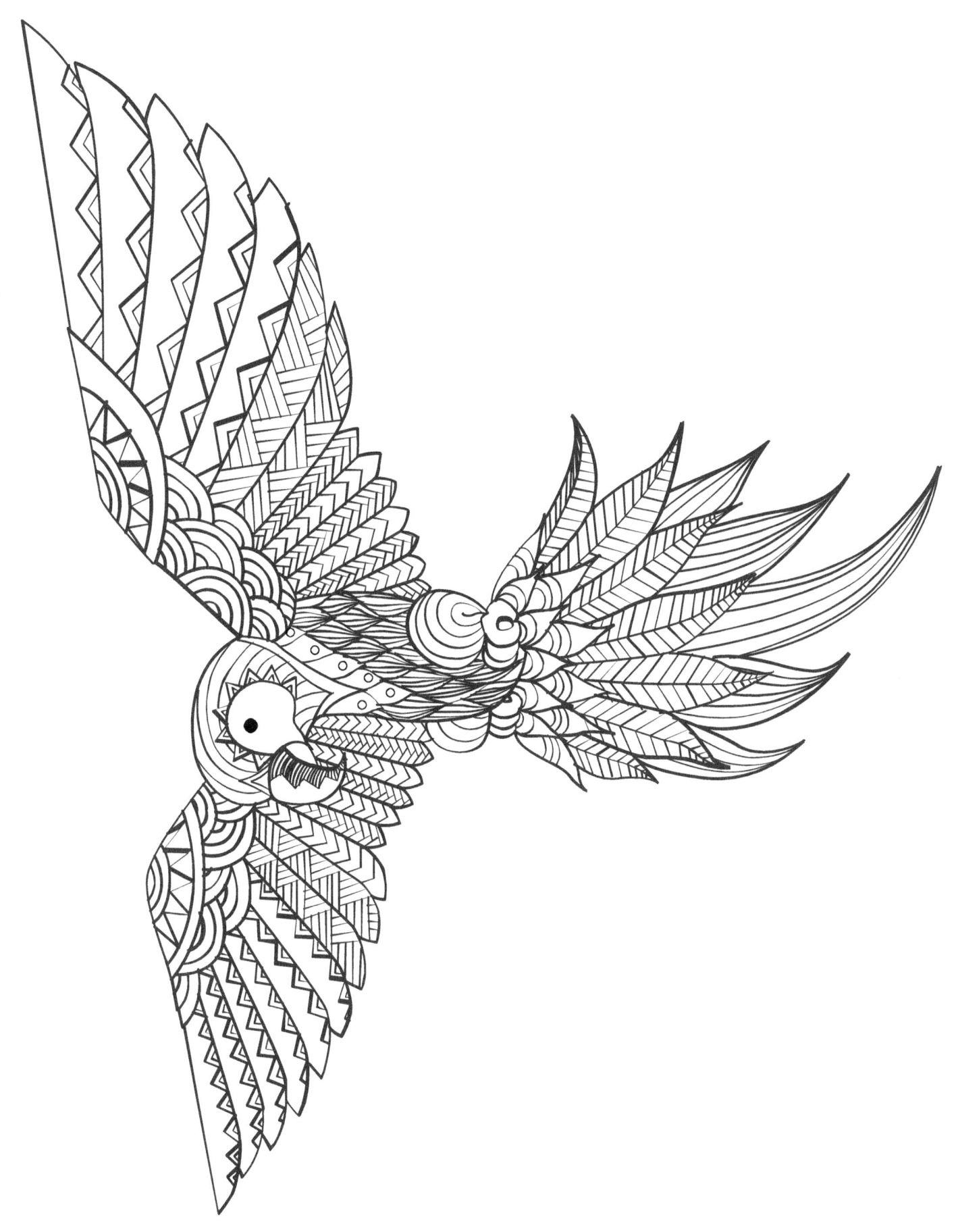

Intentionally blank

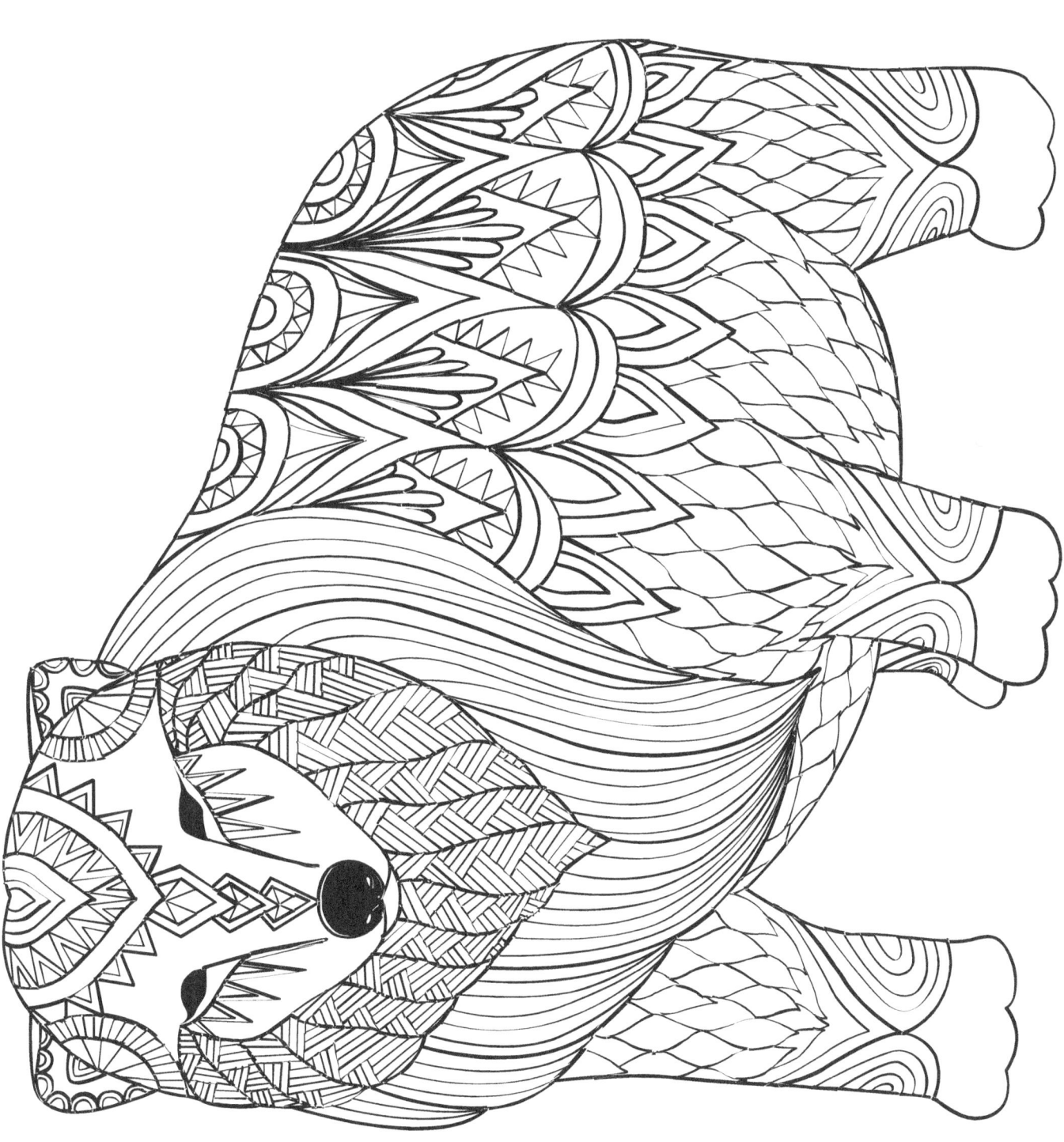

Intentionally blank

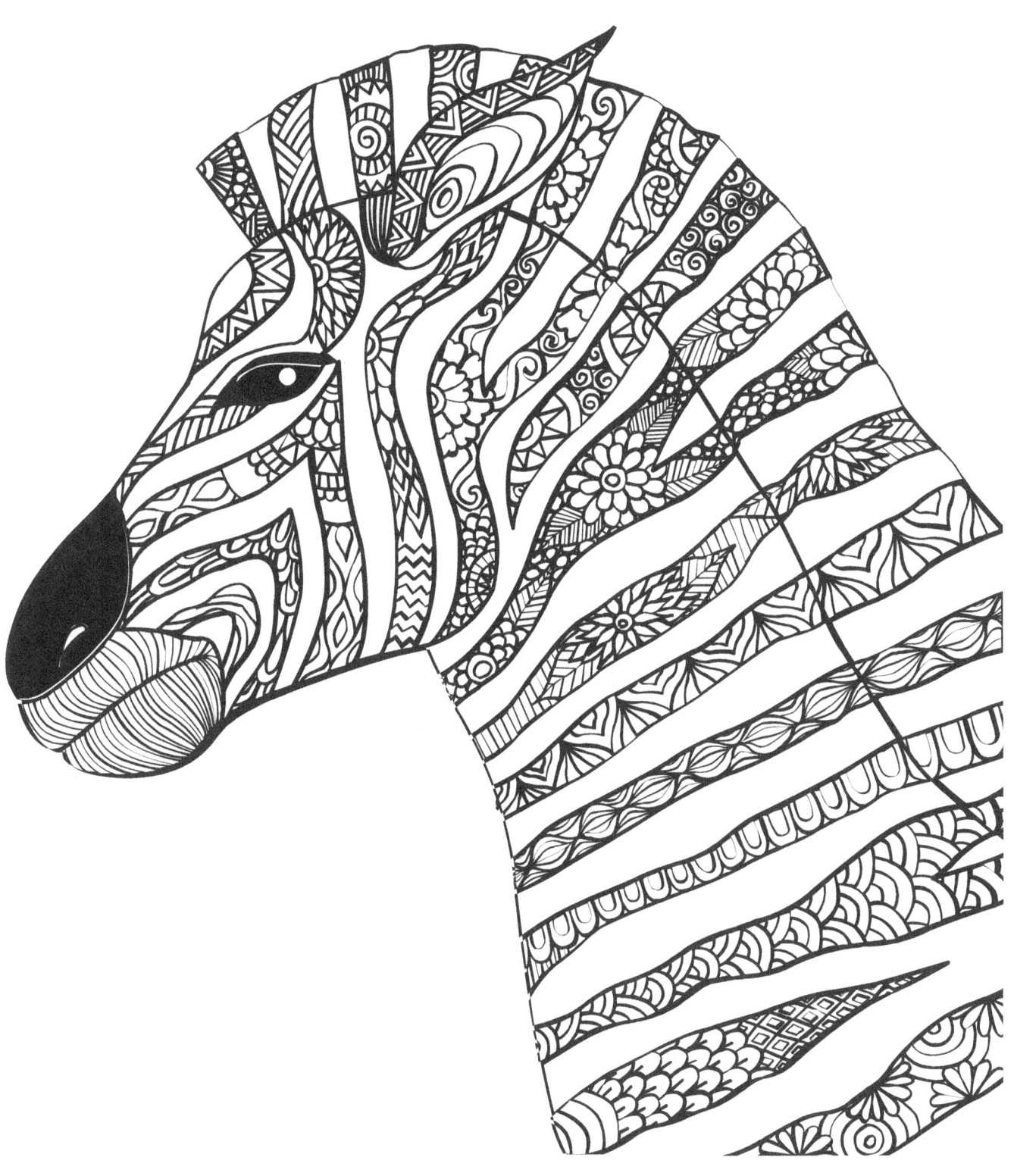

Intentionally blank

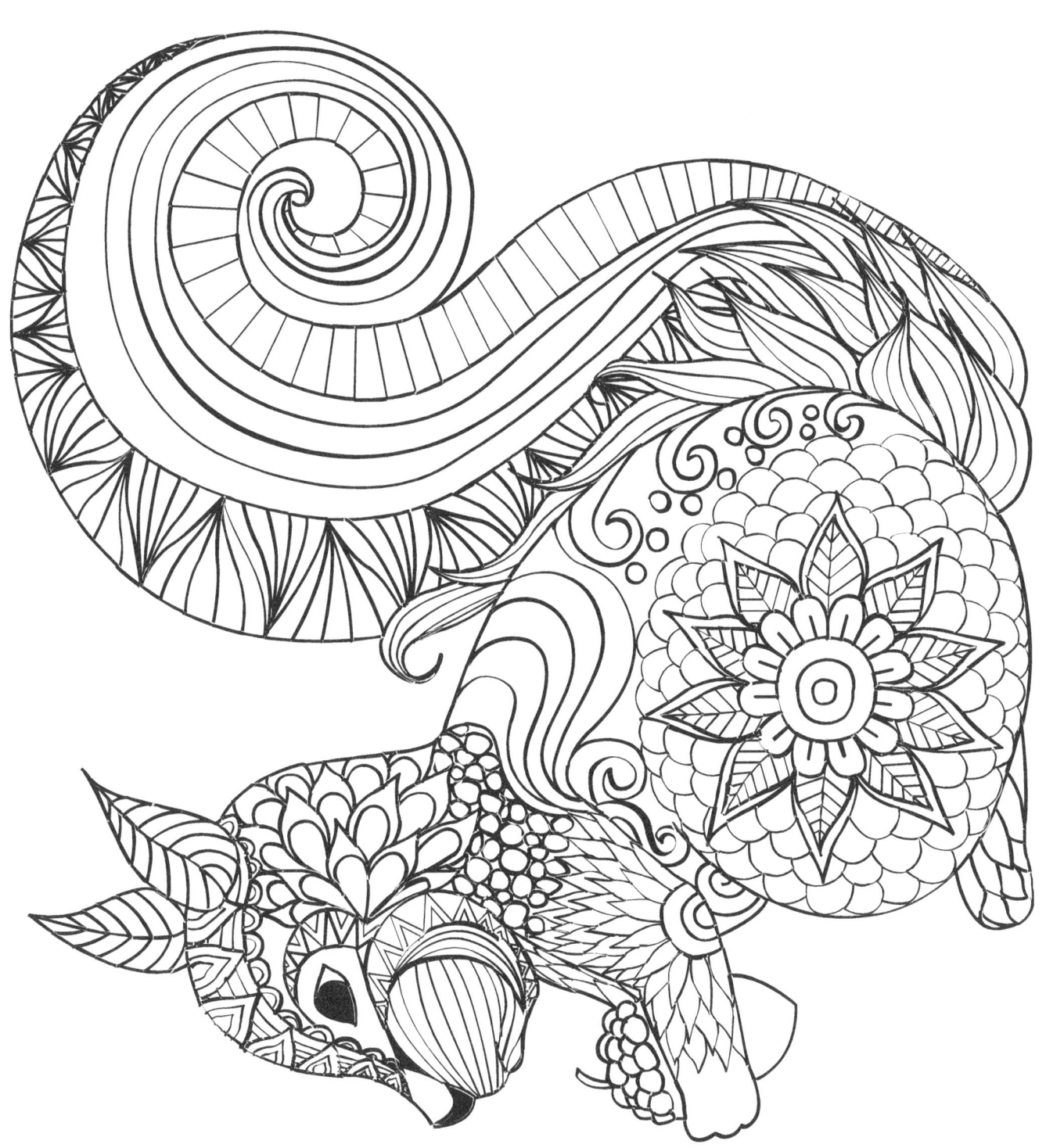

Intentionally blank

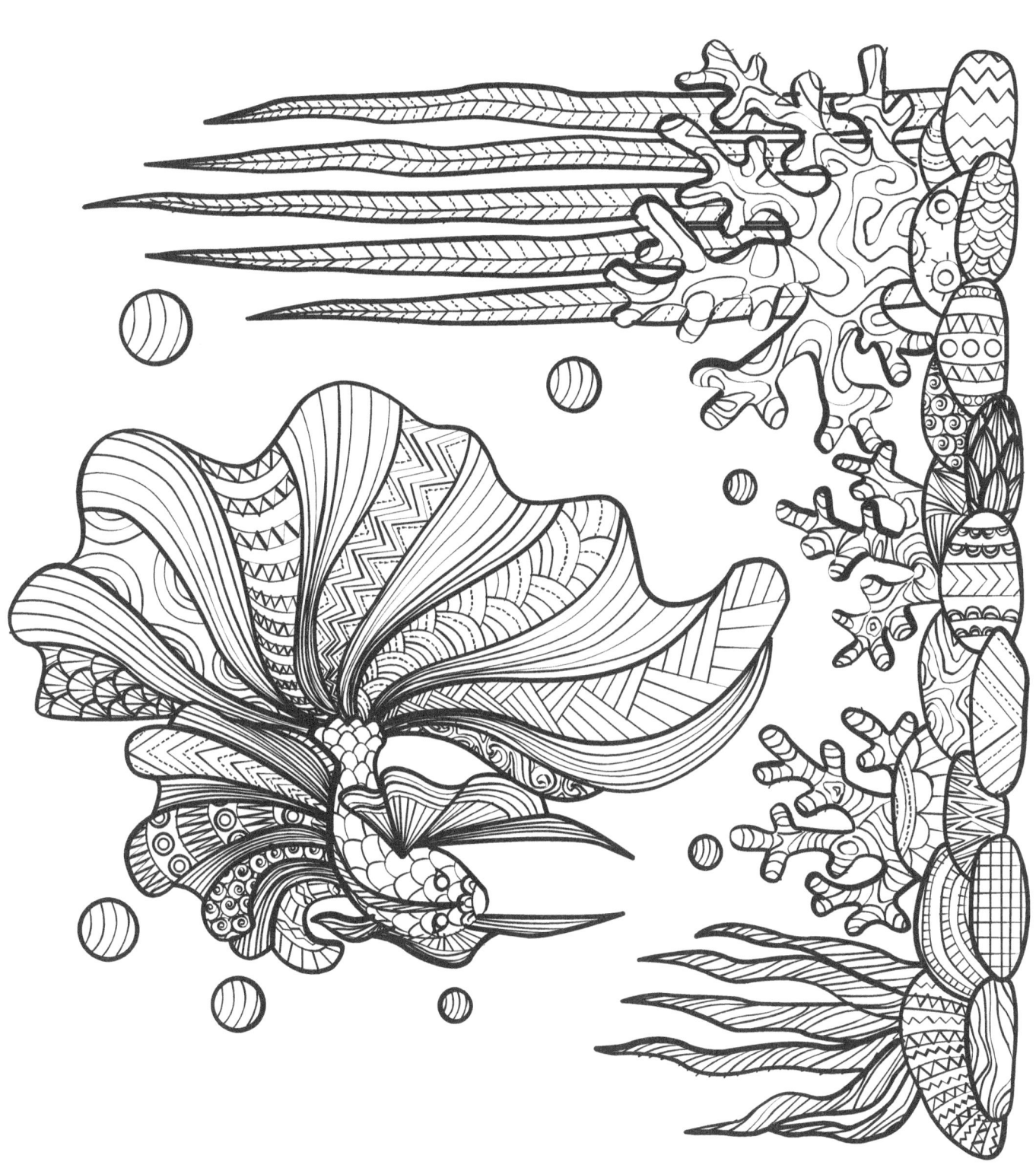

Intentionally blank

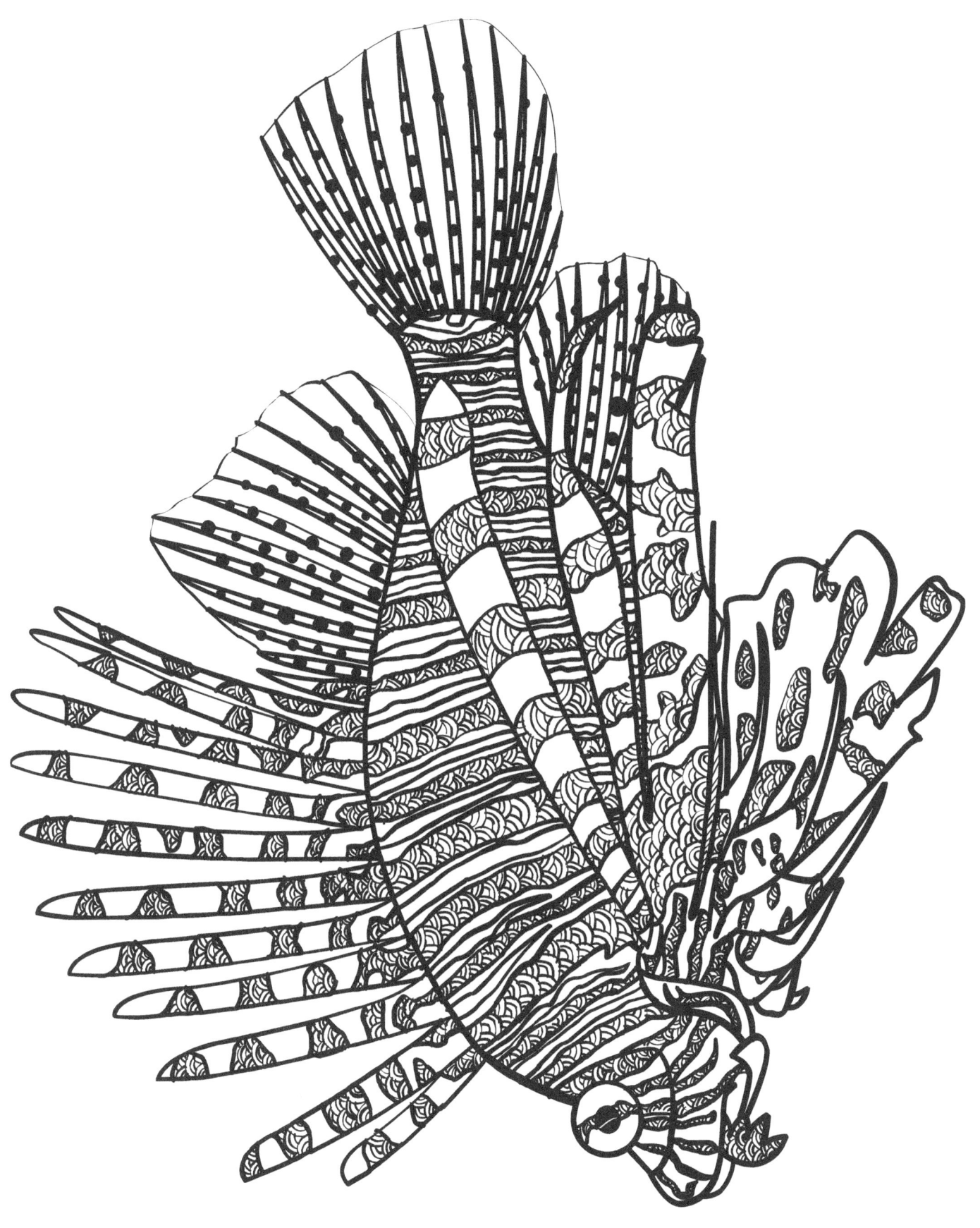

Intentionally blank

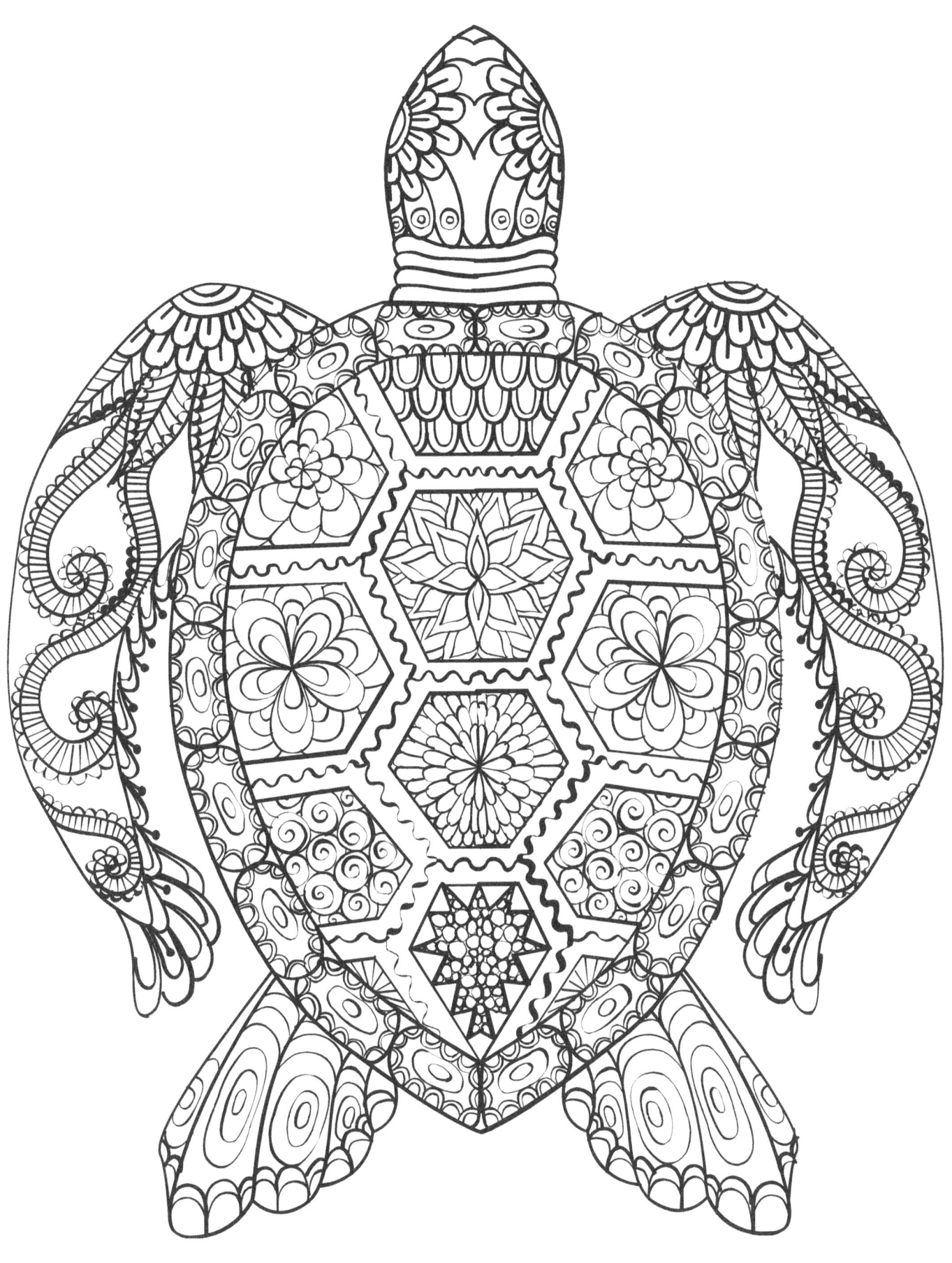

Intentionally blank

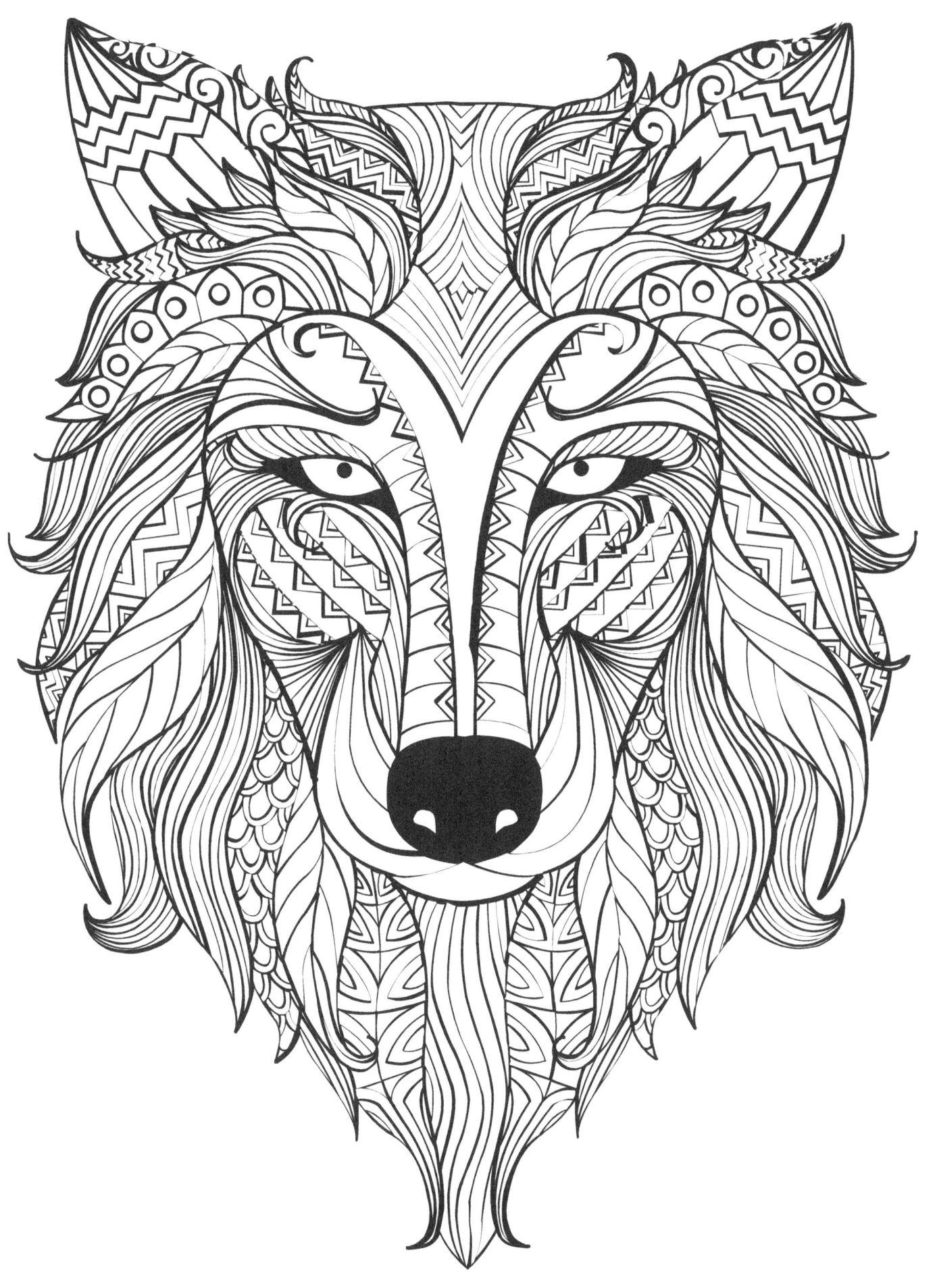

Intentionally blank

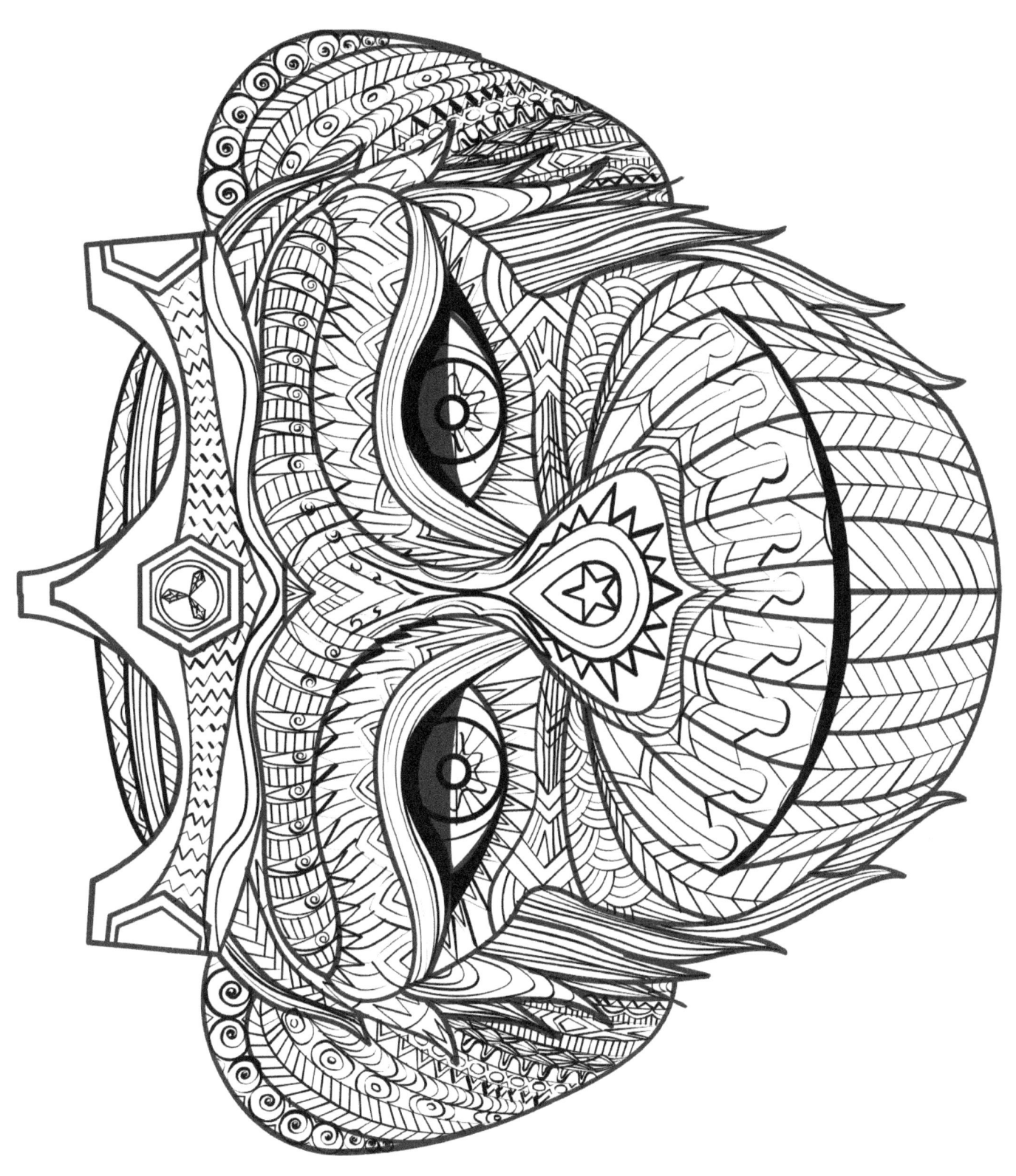

Intentionally blank

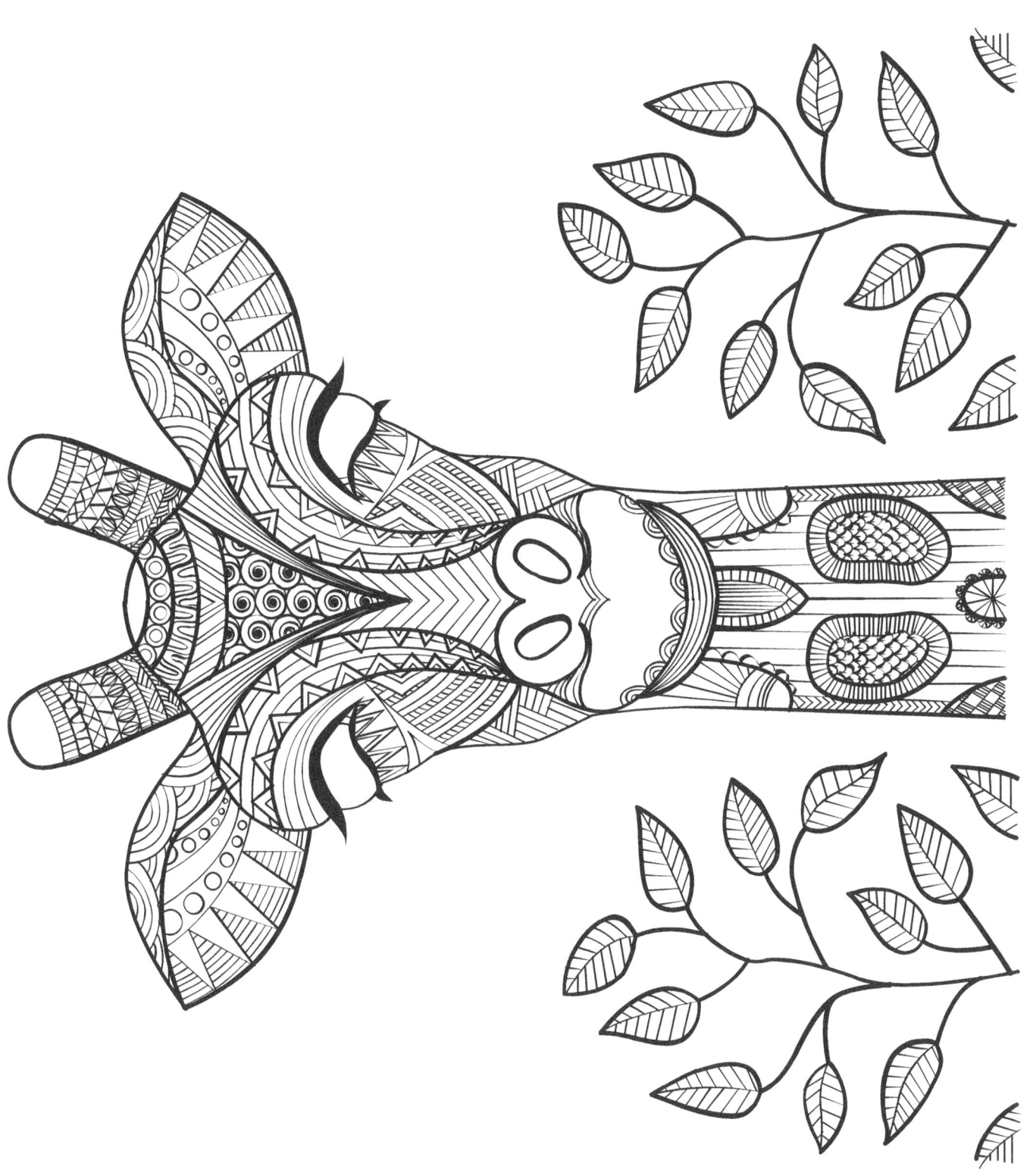

Intentionally blank

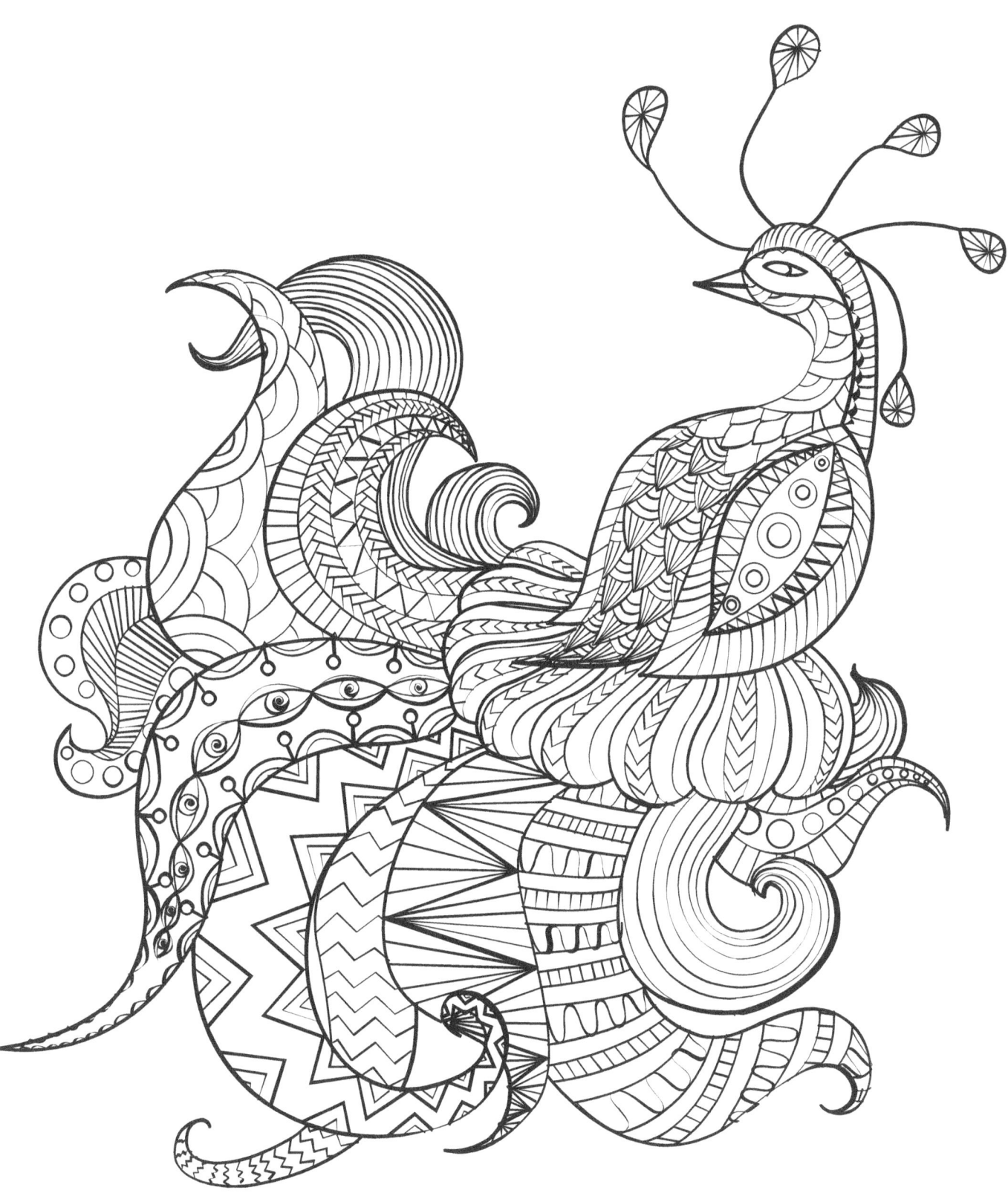

Intentionally blank

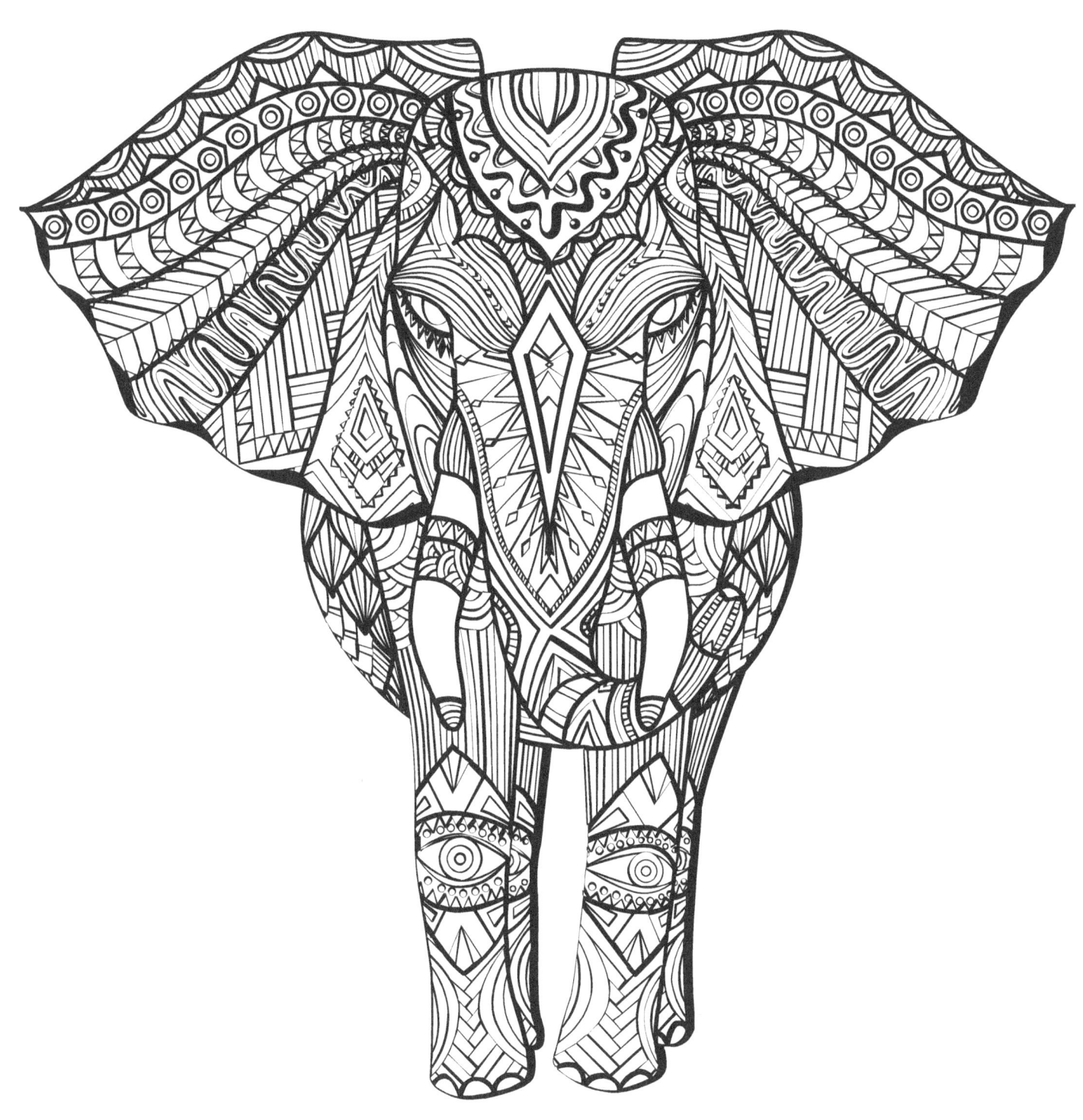

Intentionally blank

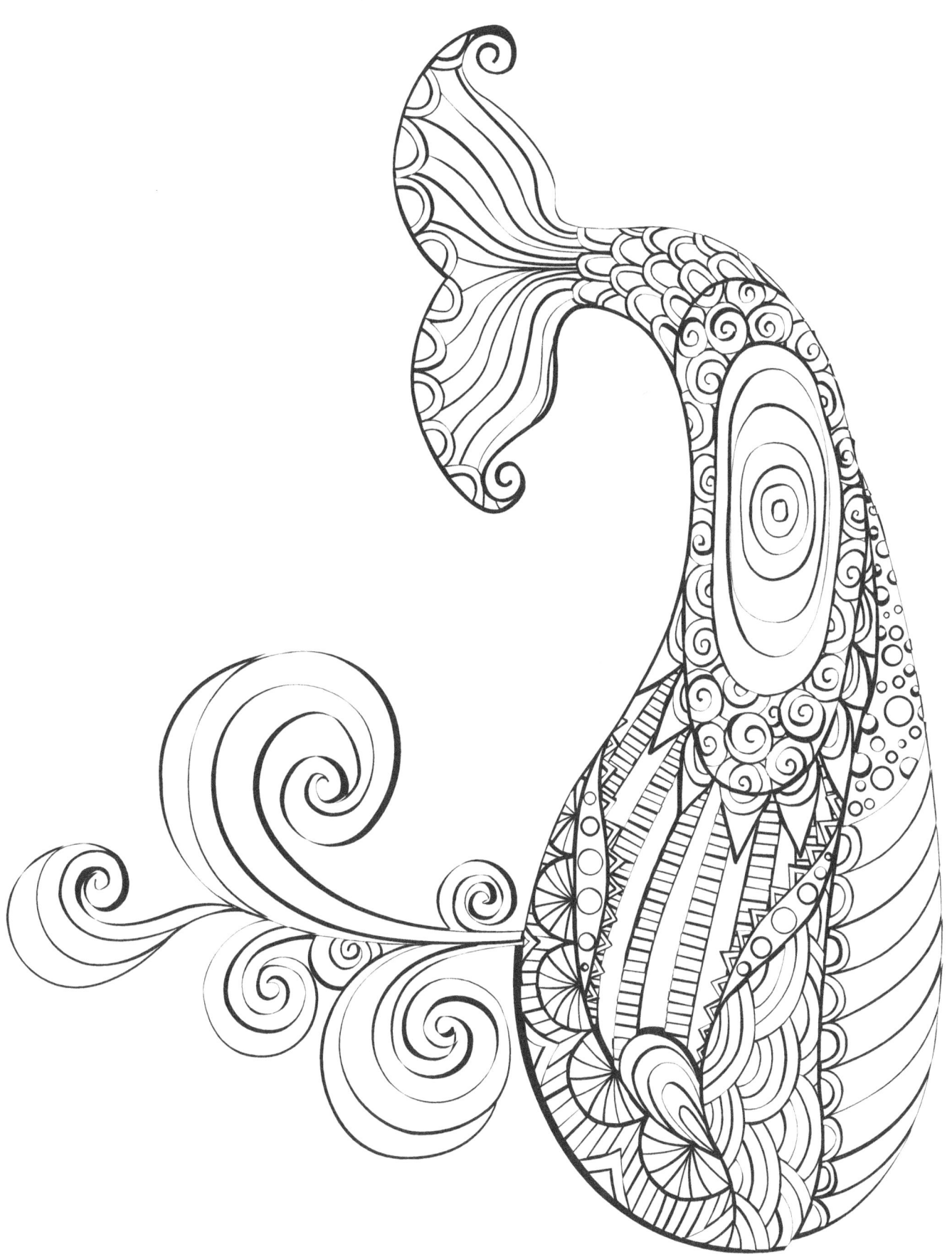

Intentionally blank

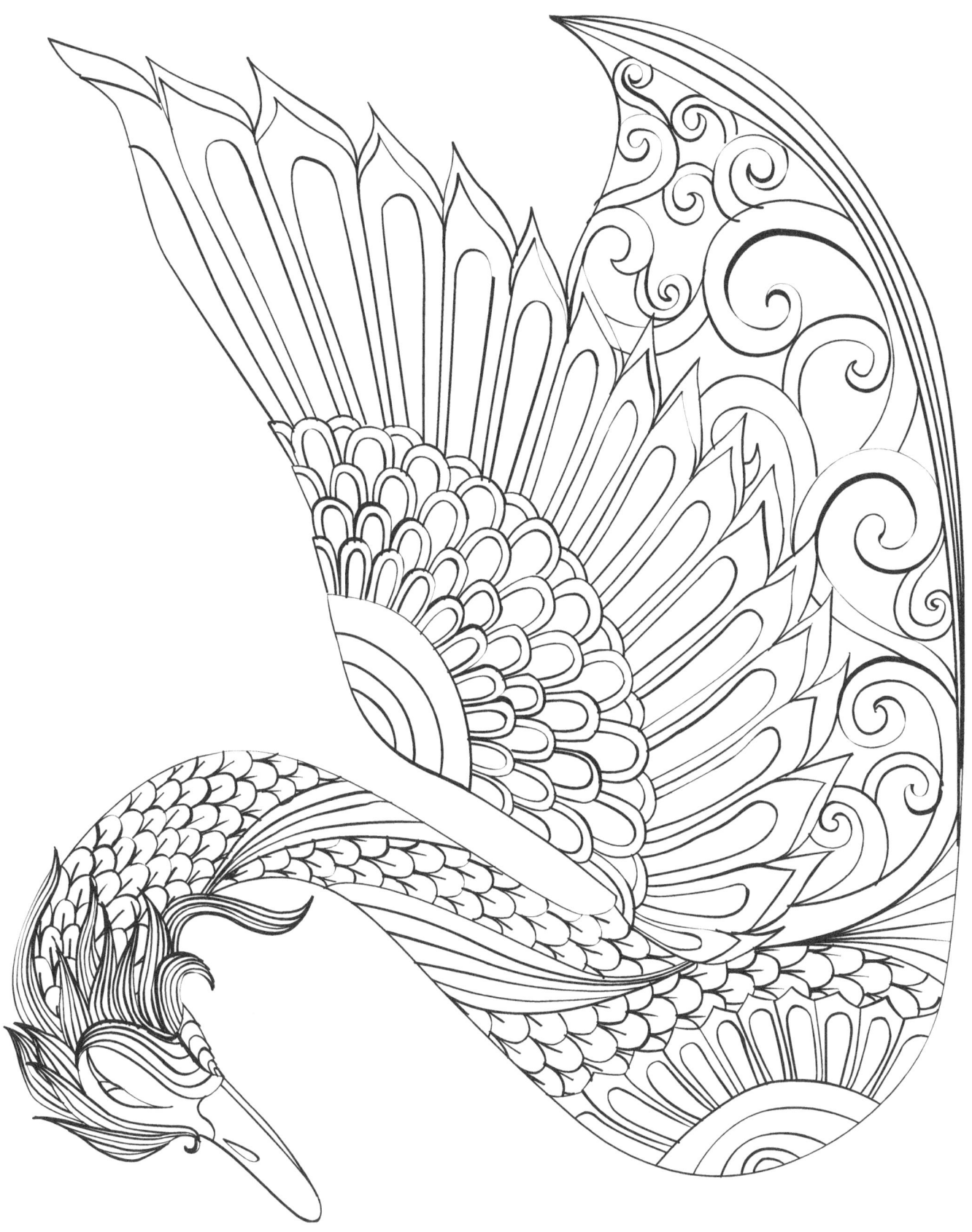

Intentionally blank

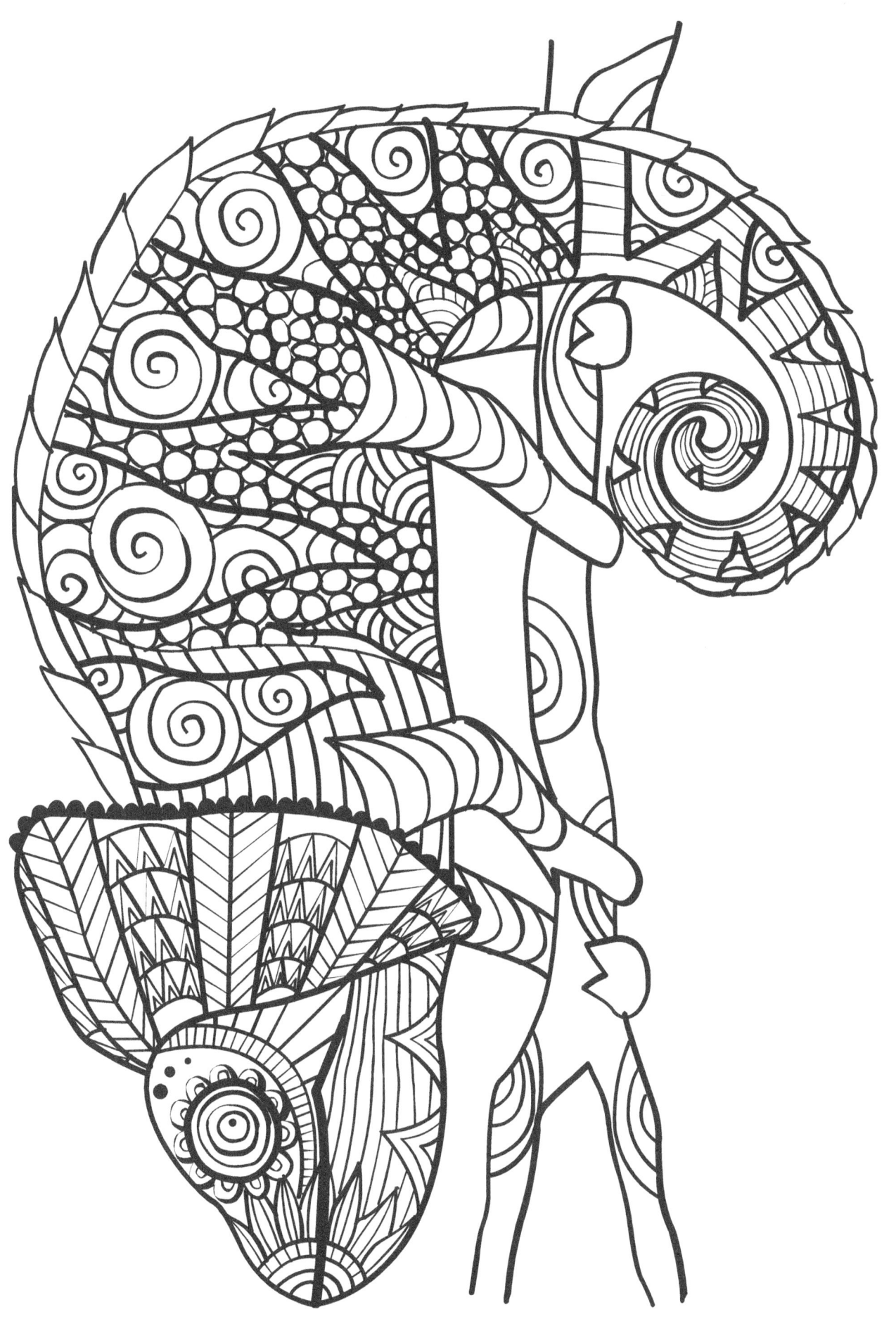

Intentionally blank

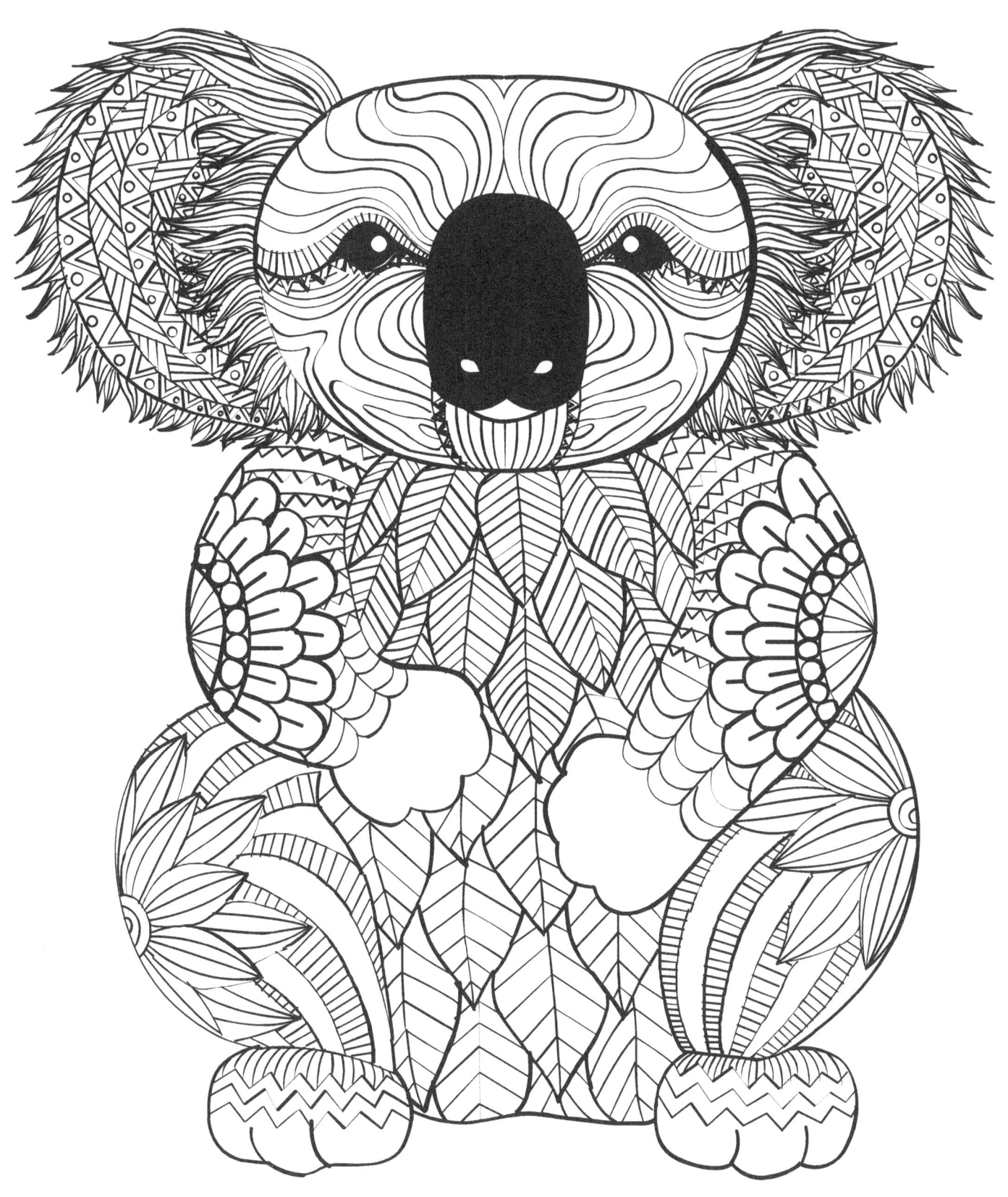

Intentionally blank

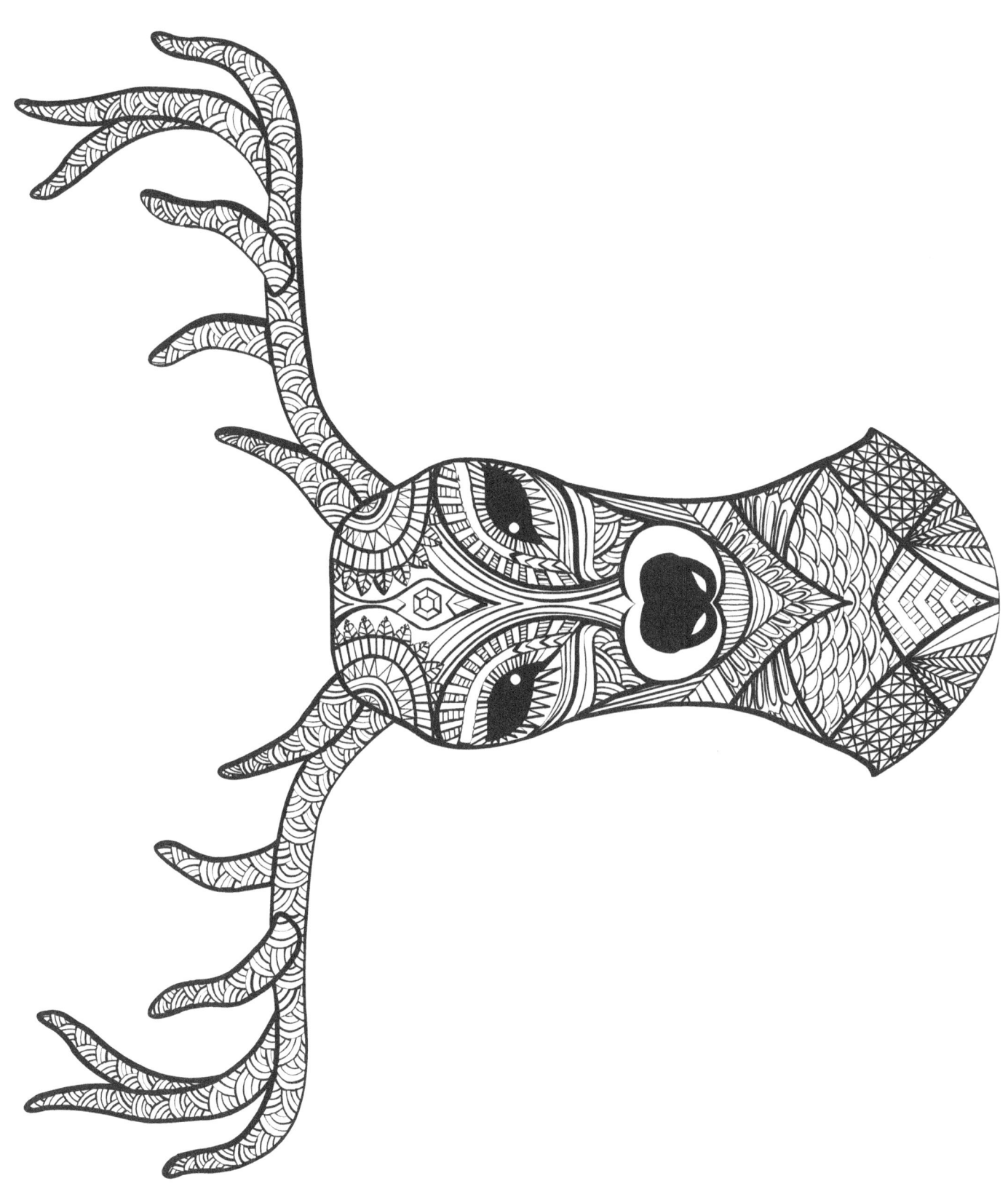

Intentionally blank

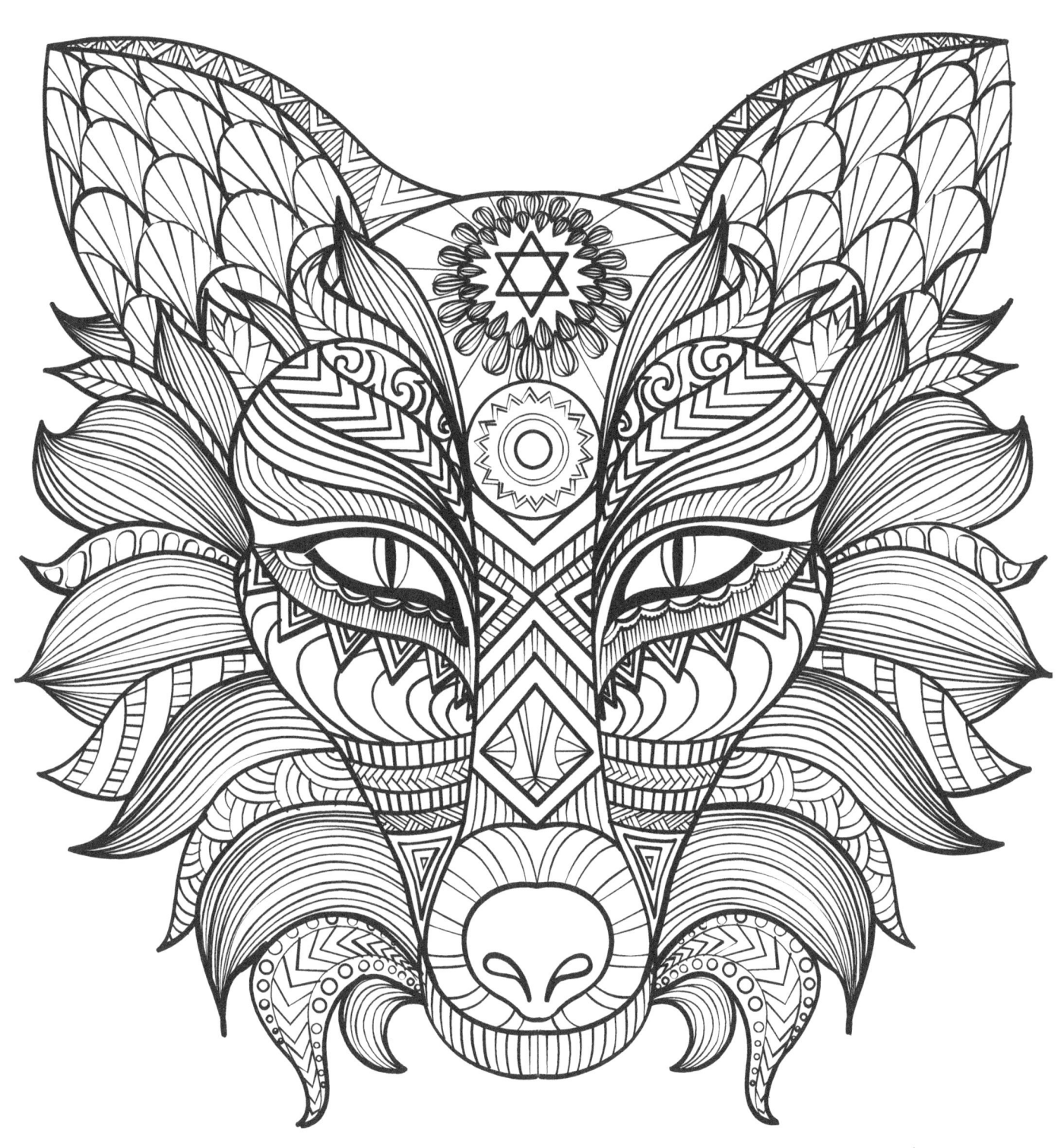

Intentionally blank

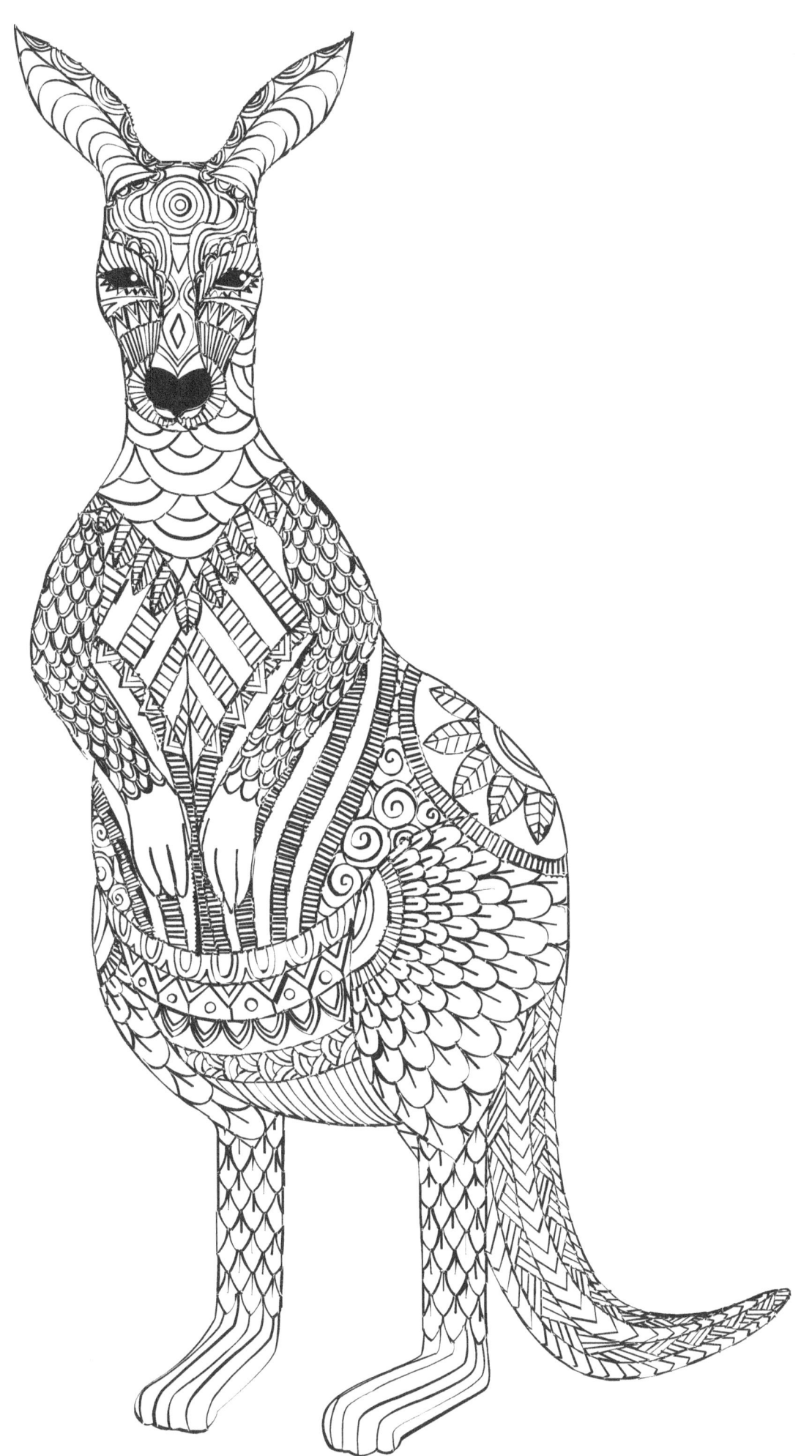